# Have You Ever Seen a Boomerang?

By JBus
Illustrated by Bindi Lee Day

We respect and honour Aboriginal and Torres Strait Islander Elders past, present and future. We acknowledge the stories, traditions and living cultures of Aboriginal and Torres Strait Islander peoples on this land and commit to building a brighter future together.

Library For All Ltd.

# boomerang

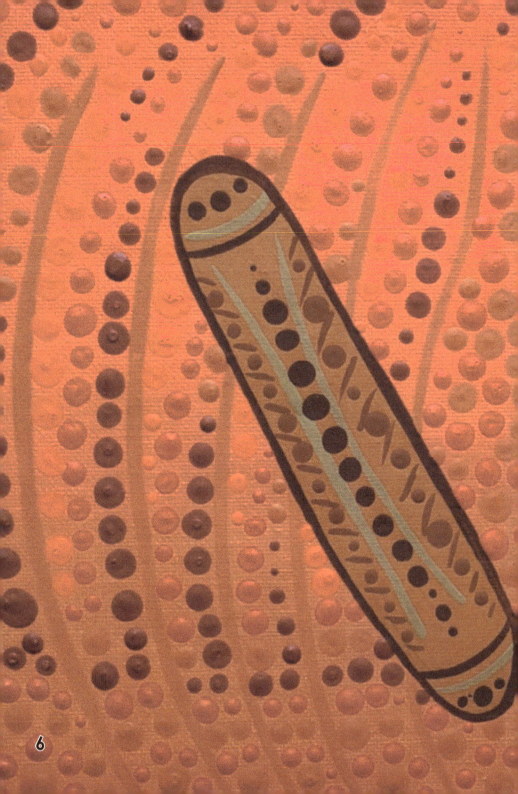

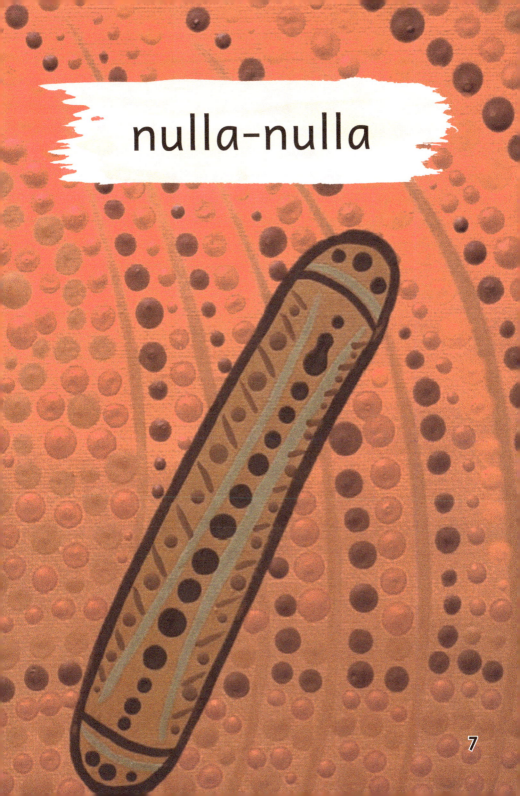
# nulla-nulla

coolamon

net

coolamon

net

# dilly bag

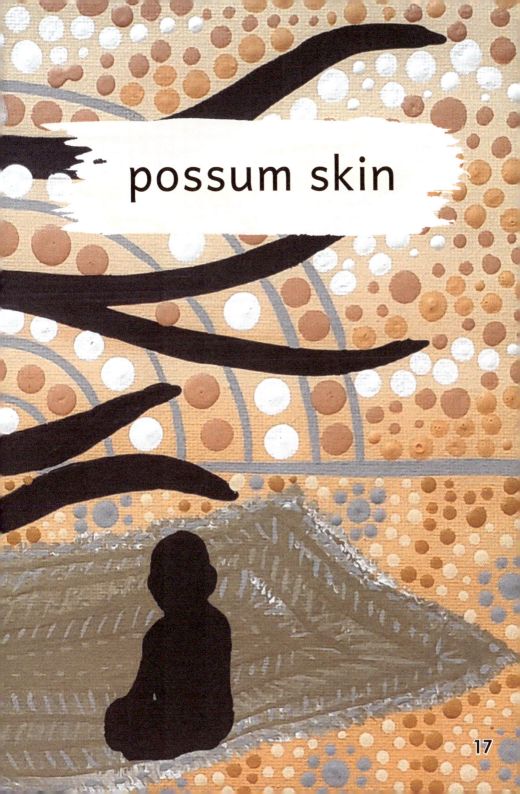

stone

What are these things used for?

**boomerang** - for hunting, digging and ceremonial dances

**clapsticks** - for making music and sharing stories

**nulla-nulla** - for hunting (usually a tool for women)

**coolamon** - for carrying food or water

**net** - for fishing or carrying food

**dilly bag** - for gathering food, like bush tucker

**lap lap** - a waistcloth, often worn for ceremonial dances by men and boys

**possum skin** - for cloaks or baby blankets and added to each year as they grow

**stone** - for grinding seeds and spices

**spear** - for hunting and ceremonial dances

**You can use these questions to talk about this book with your family, friends and teachers.**

What did you learn from this book?

Describe this book in one word. Funny? Scary? Colourful? Interesting?

How did this book make you feel when you finished reading it?

What was your favourite part of this book?

Download the Library For All Reader app from libraryforall.org

## About the contributors

JBus is a Gubbi Gubbi woman from Queensland who lives in Brisbane. She enjoys being at the beach with her family, creating art, and singing.

Bindi is a Noonuccal artist from Quandamooka country in South-East Queensland. Bindi's artistic journey has been marked by a modern style infused with storytelling that not only reflects her saltwater cultural roots but also pays homage to freshwater communities, forged through years of collaboration with traditional Aboriginal artists in central Australia.

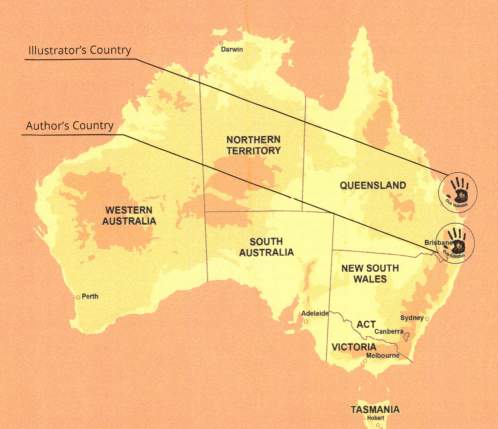

## Our Yarning

The Our Yarning collection aligns with the Australian Curriculum through the Cross-Curriculum Priorities — Aboriginal and Torres Strait Islander Histories and Cultures. The collection provides an authentic opportunity for learning and embedding Aboriginal and Torres Strait Islander perspectives because it is written by Aboriginal and Torres Strait Islander people.

We know that children learn better, and enjoy reading more, when they see themselves in the stories, characters and illustrations of the books they read.

To download the app, visit the Google Play Store or Apple Store and search 'Our Yarning'.

libraryforall.org

# You're reading Learner

## Learner – Beginner readers
Start your reading journey with short words, big ideas and plenty of pictures.

## Level 1 – Rising readers
Raise your reading level with more words, simple sentences and exciting images.

## Level 2 – Eager readers
Enjoy your reading time with familiar words, but complex sentences.

## Level 3 – Progressing readers
Develop your reading skills with creative stories and some challenging vocabulary.

## Level 4 – Fluent readers
Step up your reading skills with playful narratives, new words and fun facts.

## Middle Primary – Curious readers
Discover your world through science and stories.

## Upper Primary – Adventurous readers
Explore your world through science and stories.

Library For All is an Australian not for profit organisation with a mission to make knowledge accessible to all via an innovative digital library solution. Visit us at libraryforall.org

Have You Ever Seen a Boomerang?

First published 2024

Published by Library For All Ltd
Email: info@libraryforall.org
URL: libraryforall.org

This work is licensed under the Creative Commons Attribution-NonCommercial-NoDerivatives 4.0 International License. To view a copy of this license, visit http://creativecommons.org/licenses/by-nc-nd/4.0/.

Our Yarning logo design by Jason Lee, Bidjipidji Art

Original illustrations by Bindi Lee Day

Have You Ever Seen a Boomerang?
JBus
ISBN: 978-1-923339-64-4
SKU04553